are we there yet?

Travel  time

Where are these travelers going?
Match the people waiting in the ticket line with their destination. Use the objects that the people are carrying and their clothing as clues.

1___
2___
3___
4___
5___
6___
7___
8___
9___

TICKETS

DESTINATIONS

A
B
C
D
E
F
G
H
I

Picture Park

Can you find 22 words hidden in the tree? Look across, up, down, backwards, and diagonally. All the words listed below are pictured on this page.

dog
ice cream
bench
trees
blanket
runners
squirrel
bicycle

fishing pole
basketball
fountain
kite
pond
watermelon
flowers

slide
picnic
teeter-totter
radio
swing set
cooler
duck

```
            R I B F
      A I C E C R E A M
    W D T R T E O E N D
    I O A E T T S I O P C L
    G A N T R O T D A L B H
    B A S K E T B A L L E D N
    N F L O W E R S R A O U R S
    S I T H R S E M N E C R W I
    S L A N U I T K E K T I S K
    Q I T N P E L F L N A I C
    E U D N T E L I G O T I I
    I E U T N S N E N A
    E R U O E H P O N D
    S R T F I
    E E N G
    P L C P
    I C Y O
    C Y C L
    N C I E
    I B X
    C
```

The bugs at your picnic have a message for you. Use the key to fill in the blanks.

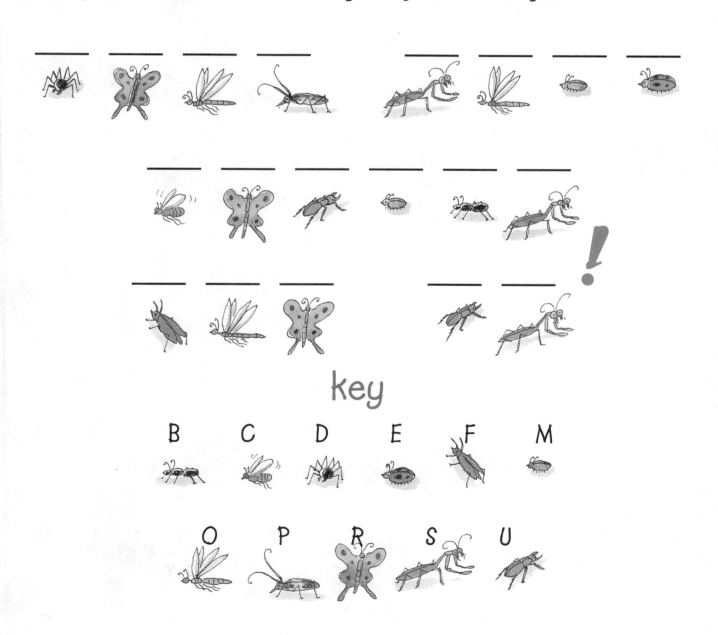

key

B   C   D   E   F   M

O   P   R   S   U

Souvenir
dot-to-dot

Mom brought home a souvenir from her trip to New York City.
Connect the dots in order from 1 to 71 to find out what it is.

Headline Adventure

Create your own wacky news story.
Ask somebody for words to fill in the blanks below. Then read the story aloud.

It was a _____ night and the _____ family was driving down the highway on their
      ADJECTIVE (describing word)   NAME

way to _____. All of a sudden, they saw _____ _____ along the side of the
      PLACE   NUMBER   PLURAL NOUN

highway. They decided to _____ because it seemed like the right thing to do.
                   VERB

_____ decided to call for a little _____ and everyone else started _____.
  NAME   NOUN   -ING WORD

When the _____ arrived, everything was under control. A passerby said, "It certainly was lucky
      NOUN

that this _____ family was driving by. Those kids knew exactly what to do
      ADJECTIVE (describing word)

in a _____ like this. The kids admitted, "We were _____, and it was a great adventure,
    NOUN   ADJECTIVE (describing word)

but now we have to get _____."
              -ING WORD

Travel Journal

Today is _____ I am in _____

Best thing I did today _____

Worst thing I did today _____

Other Stuff

FUN-O-METER
Today is...

FUN

NOT

words fail!
totally AWESOME
Cool
Pretty FUN
OK
zero fun
BIG PAIN

MOOD ChecK
Today I feel...

☐ Cheerful
☐ Helpful
☐ Homesick
☐ Dopey
☐ Grumpy
☐ Sleepy
☐ Bashful
☐ Silly
☐ Bored
☐ Other

2B continued

Weather or Not
Today's weather is...

Travel tips

Here are some tips to get you started.

Stake out your territory.

Show off your map reading skills.

Now try your own.

Stay energized!

Summer Vacation Crossword Puzzle

ACROSS

1. Pool of rain in the street
4. Wheeled plank that "surfs" on sidewalk
9. Car without a roof
12. Short-sleeved cotton garment
14. Grassy area around a house
15. Napping spot that swings between two trees
17. Person who polices the beach
18. Inner_____(fun float toy)
19. Crashing breakers at the ocean
21. Grass-watering sprayer
22. Rose or daisy_____

DOWN

1. Spiced cucumber sometimes eaten on hamburgers
2. Plunging into a pool off the board
3. Serving of corn on the cob
4. Water_____("ride" behind a boat)
5. Play home in the branches
6. Umpire's word in baseball
7. What to do when you're thirsty
8. Large, seedy summer fruit
10. Sport played with rackets and a net
11. To grill meat
13. Provides shade at the beach
16. Results of sitting in the sun
18. What to sit on at the beach
20. To jump rope

Picture Postcard

On one side of the postcard, draw a picture from your trip.
On the other side, write all about it.

To: _____
_____
_____
_____

Can you find 30 things in this scene that start with the letter T?
Finding 15 is tricky, 20 is terrific, and 25 or more is tip-top.

Make me a map

The mapmaker has fallen asleep on the job. She drew 15 states but forgot to label them. Can you match the states with their names?

1. Florida _____

2. Michigan _____

3. Oklahoma _____

4. Ohio _____

5. Louisiana _____

6. California _____

7. Hawaii _____

8. Nevada _____

9. Virginia _____

10. Tennessee _____

11. Washington _____

12. New York _____

13. Utah _____

14. Massachusetts _____

15. Idaho _____

A B C D E F G H I J K L M N O

This car needs a tune up. Can you unscramble the 14 parts listed below?

1. STRINGEE LEWEH _____
2. HODO _____
3. LACEORCRATE _____
4. KNURT _____
5. SWINDLEHID _____
6. BAKER _____
7. BRASHADDO _____
8. HEWEL _____
9. RIGHTSAFE _____
10. GENNIE _____
11. LADHEIGHT _____
12. BURPEM _____
13. ELFMURF _____
14. TYRETAB _____

Something's Fishy

Can you spot 10 differences between the top and bottom fish tanks?

Surf's Up!

Can you find 10 things wrong with this picture?

Travel log

Write your own "been there, done that" lists under the headings below.

I've **Been There**

I've **DONE THAT**

I'D **LIKE TO GO THERE**

I **NEVER** want to go there.

Wacky Water Park

Call the lifeguard! There's a whale in the swimming pool. That's not the only thing wrong at this water park. Look at the picture to find 11 other strange things.

On the right track

The 19 words listed below are hidden in the train. Look across, back, up, down, and diagonally to find them.

BOXCAR
BRAKEMAN
CABOOSE
CARGO
CATTLECAR
CHOO-CHOO
CONDUCTOR
CROSSING
ENGINEER
EXPRESS
LOCOMOTIVE
MONORAIL
PULLMAN
RAILROAD
ROUNDHOUSE
SIGNAL
TIES
TUNNEL
WHISTLE

```
            T R N       L R A           S T P U
            O A C       O C A           I O U L
            L E M O L R C E A I B Y A S M B
            S E I T H T O S N R L R L O A O X
            K A N I N C M S S G G R N O N X
I S A R O U N D H O U S E I O O B T C
O R S C O N D U C T O R I R N E A E A L
B W H I S T L E T I I H A N P E C D R
R A C E L T T A C V F I C E G X E A
    G A T       H E L       A E R
    C H R       I S T       I E
```

b l o o m e r s

How many flowers can you name using the word pictures below?

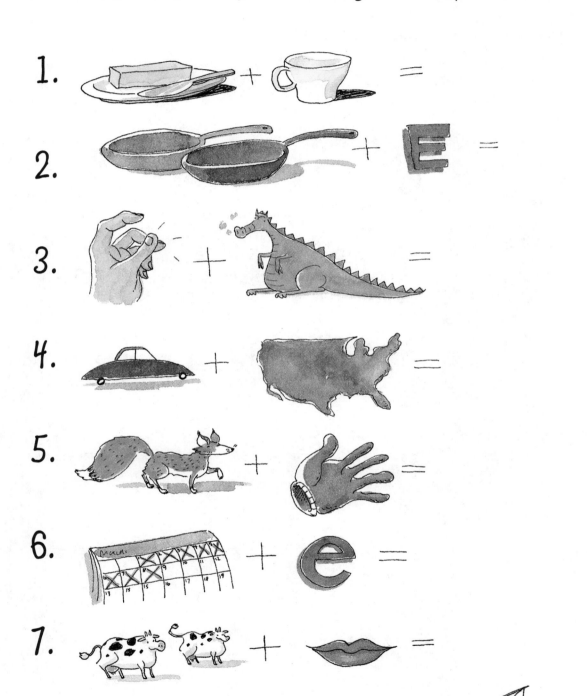

1.   ☐ + ☐ =

2.   ☐ + **E** =

3.   ☐ + ☐ =

4.   ☐ + ☐ =

5.   ☐ + ☐ =

6.   ☐ + **e** =

7.   ☐ + ☐ =

8.   ☐ + **N** + ☐ =

Pathways

Juan wants to go fishing, Michelle wants to do some bird watching, and Keisha wants to go rock climbing. Which trail should each person take?

Winter Vacation Crossword Puzzle

ACROSS

1. Hanukkah and Thanksgiving are two
4. Sled-pulling dog
8. Apple drink
10. Light coat
11. Pine trees, for instance
16. Head covering
18. Wax with a wick
19. Warm fabric for sheets or pajamas
20. Bed covering
21. Where to burn logs indoors
22. Twinkling light in the sky
23. Container that keeps drinks hot
24. The North _____ (Santa's home)

DOWN

1. Game played with a puck
2. Cozy inn
3. To glide on ice with blades
4. Sweet, warm drink
5. Frosty, for instance
6. Holiday word with log or -tide
7. downhill or cross-country gliders
9. Floor covering
12. Rudolph, for instance
13. Travel on a snowmobile
14. Warm, knitted pullover
15. Sledded carrier pulled by horses
17. Hibernating

Highway Robbery

It was late in the afternoon as we sped along the dusty road in the family station wagon. We were on our way to Florida for our annual family vacation and my little sister Louise was really starting to get on my nerves. We were nearly to Chattanooga when the station wagon slowed down.

"What's going on?" my mother asked.

Through the windshield I could see some sort of road-block. We slowly crept along until we reached several police officers standing by orange cones that blocked the road. An old blue convertible had been directed over to the side of the road and one of the officers was talking with the man who owned it.

My dad rolled down his window as another police officer approached our car.

"There's been a robbery at the local grocery store ten miles away," the officer explained. "We're checking cars because we think the robber is trying to get out of town."

We all got out of the car. I sat on the bumper, listening to the conversation between the other policeman and the man in the blue convertible. I noticed that his backseat was filled with grocery bags.

"Officer, I tell you, these are my things I bought a day ago in Salt Lake City," the man said. I've been driving for 12 hours straight. I haven't even heard of the grocery store you're talking about."

The policeman looked skeptical. He strolled to the front of the car, took out a notepad, and began writing down the license plate number on the convertible.

The man was not telling the truth. Do you know what gave him away?

Happy Camper?

Help make this hungry camper a happy camper. Find the hidden fork, plate, cup, cooler, sandwich, apple, bottle of juice, and slice of cake.

Under the Big Top

Connect the dots in order from 1 to 109 to find out what the girl is riding.

Message in the sand

Your friends have left you a note on the beach. Use the key to fill in the blanks.

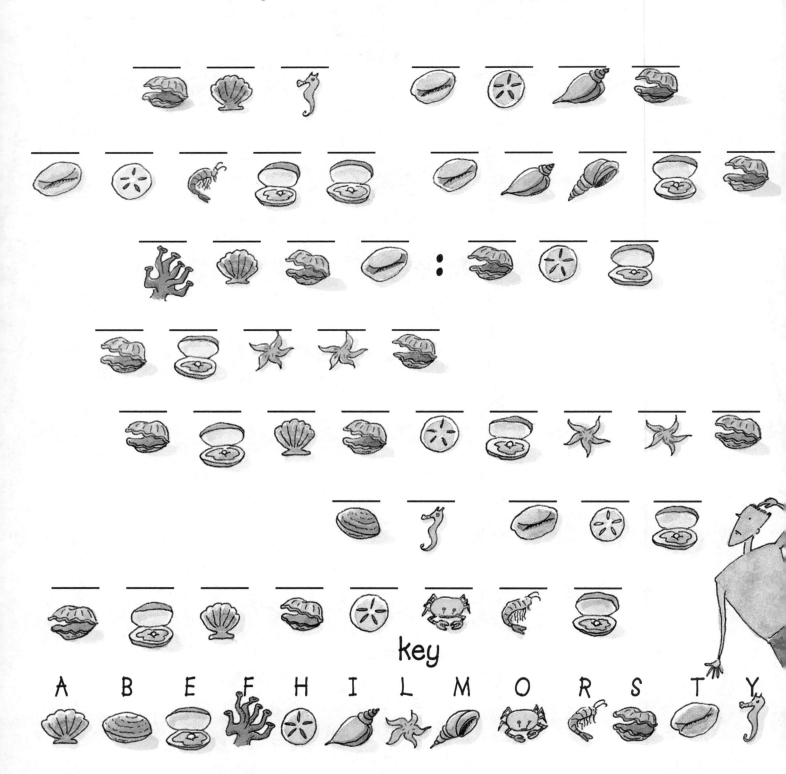

key

A   B   E   F   H   I   L   M   O   R   S   T   Y

Barnyard Scramble

How many of the 14 animal names can you unscramble?
All of the animals are pictured on this page.

1. GDO _____
2. ACT _____
3. OWC _____
4. ADOT _____
5. KUCD _____
6. TOGA _____
7. ORCW _____

8. OGSOE _____
9. EOMUS _____
10. SHOER _____
11. NOBRI _____
12. BRITAB _____
13. NARCOCO _____
14. RLIQEUSR _____

Backseat Bingo

binjo!

This game can be played with up to four people. Select a bingo card. Each time you see one of the items pictured on the card, draw an X on that square. The first person to cross out five squares across, down, or diagonally wins.

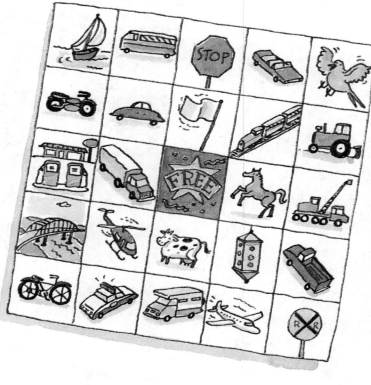

Wait for me!

Your friends have run off to their favorite rides at the amusement park.
Use the nine squares below as hints to help you find your friends.

Bumper Cars

Tons O' Fun
amusement park

Travel Journal

Today is _____   I am in _____

What I like about this place _____

What I don't like _____

Other Stuff

FUN-O-METER
Today is...

- words fail!
- totally AWESOME
- Cool
- Pretty FUN
- OK
- zero fun
- BIG PAIN

FUN
NOT

MOOD Check
Today I feel...

- ☐ Thoughtful
- ☐ Carefree
- ☐ Careless
- ☐ Sporty
- ☐ Jolly
- ☐ Goofy
- ☐ Witty
- ☐ Friendly
- ☐ Unfriendly
- ☐ Other

2B continued

Weather or Not
Today's weather is...

Fantasy Vacation

What's the best vacation *you* can imagine? Maybe it's sailing on the ocean, racing down the slopes, or even blasting off into space. Draw a picture of your very own fantasy vacation below.

Start pedaling in Cape Cod, Massachusetts,
and coast across the finish line in California.
Watch out!, There might be a few dead ends in your path.

The race is On!

Start

Movie Set Match-up

There has been a mix-up on the movie set. See if you can help by matching the actors with their vehicles. Use the objects that the actors are carrying and their clothes as clues.

1___
2___
3___
4___
5___
6___
7___
8___
9___
10___

A
B
C
D
E
F
G
H
I
J

PROPS

U.S. MAIL

U.S. M

NASA

Plane Challenge

See if you can find a place in the puzzle for all of the words listed below. The numbers show you how many letters are in each word. Here's a hint: Start with the words that have 12, 14, or 16 letters in them. (Spaces between words don't count!)

3
hub
nap
sky

4
gate
ramp
soda
tags

5
aisle
coach
hotel
novel
pilot
seats
snack

6
laptop
pillow
on time
snooze
ticket

7
airport
blanket
co-pilot
deplane
parking
peanuts

8
airspeed
landings
navigate
schedule
takeoffs

9
concourse
passenger

10
first class
flight plan
turbulence

11
folding tray
landing gear

12
baggage check

13
inflight movie
ticket counter

14
carry-on luggage

15
baggage carousel
crossword puzzle
flight attendant

16
cruising altitude

BicYcle Mix-up

Looks like a bicycle mix-up. Can you find 10 other things wrong with this picture?

You have exactly 205 tickets to spend on prizes. If you want to spend exactly all of your tickets and you don't want to buy more than one of anything, which items should you buy?

Which hotel?

It's getting late and the Tyred family needs to find their hotel. They know it's on Yawn Avenue, but which hotel is it? Mr. Tyred stayed here years ago and remembers the facts below. Use them to figure out where the family should check in before everyone falls asleep!

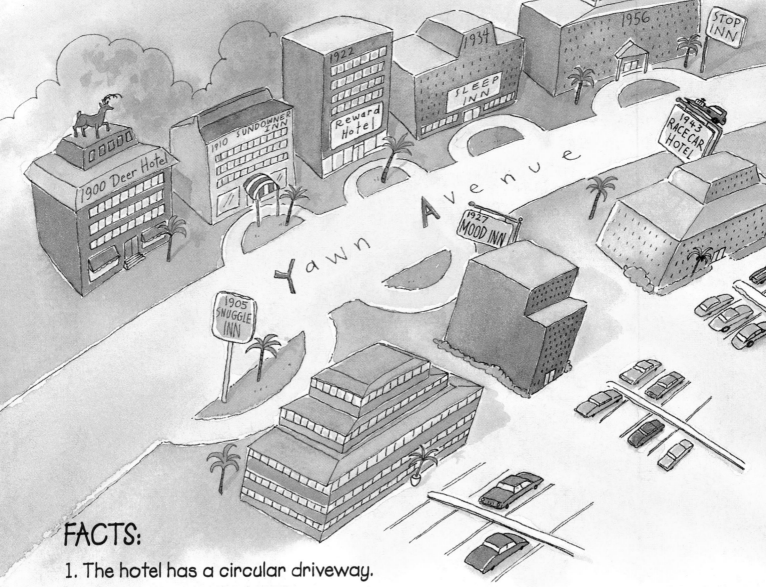

FACTS:

1. The hotel has a circular driveway.
2. The number on the hotel is even.
3. The hotel is between two hotels that have palm trees in front of them.
4. The name of the hotel (without the word "inn" or "hotel") spells another word when it is written backwards.

Zany Zoo

Can you spot 10 differences between the top and bottom scenes?

While-you-wait Bingo

This game can be played with up to four people. Select a bingo card. Each time you see one of the items pictured on the card, draw an X on that square. The first person to cross out five squares across, down, or diagonally wins.

Best vacation ever!

Create your own crazy story. Ask somebody for words to fill in the blanks below.
Then read the story aloud.

_____ says that the best vacation ever is a _____ trip to _____.
PERSON'S NAME   NOUN   PLACE

Once you're there, you just have to _____. And don't forget to _____. The most exciting
VERB   VERB

things to do are _____ and _____, but only if you're wearing _____.
ACTIVITY   ACTIVITY   TYPE OF CLOTHING

There's _____ food to eat, too. Order the _____ and _____ special
ADJECTIVE (describing word)   NOUN   NOUN

for a real treat, and tell them _____ sent you. Before you head home, be sure to buy
PERSON'S NAME

a _____ at the souvenir shop! It will always remind you of your _____ trip.
NOUN   ADJECTIVE (describing word)

Travel Journal

Today is _____   I am in _____

Here's what made me mad _____

But this made me laugh _____

Other Stuff

FUN·O·METER
Today is...

FUN ↑
NOT ↓

words fail!
totally AWESOME
cool
Pretty FUN
O.K.
zero fun
BIG PAIN

MOOD cheCK
Today I feel...

☐ Happy
☐ Lucky
☐ Happy-go-lucky
☐ Perky
☐ Pouty
☐ Stubborn
☐ Playful
☐ Naughty
☐ Nice
☐ Other

2B continued

Weather or Not
Today's weather is...

Thumbs Up / Thumbs Down

List the best of your trip on this side.

List the worst on this side.

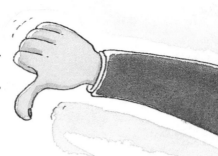

Places to go

Things to do

People I've Met

Food & Restaurants

Souvenir

official movie star glasses $5.

Soup's On

How many foods can you name using the pictures below?
You'll have to add and subtract letters or words to find the answers.

$$=$$

$$+ \bigcirc =$$

$$M + \quad - B + A + \quad + \quad + \& + \quad =$$

$$\quad - t + G + \quad - n + I =$$

$$\quad + \quad - \quad + \quad - F =$$

Stormy Seas

How many of these words can you unscramble? All 13 sea-going vessels are pictured above.

1. KAR _____
2. PISH _____
3. FRAT _____
4. OCEAN _____
5. CHATY _____
6. YAKKA _____
7. REBAG _____

8. BUGATTO _____
9. LOANDOG _____
10. ALSOBAIT _____
11. BRAINMUSE _____
12. WEIRDSNURF _____
13. CARRIFAT RICERRA _____

A few pointers

Follow the directions of the arrows in each block to find a route from go to stop.

Scattered suitcases

This conveyor belt is going too fast, and the luggage has spilled all over the floor. Can you help the musician find her headphones, harmonica, sheet music, compact discs, and horn?

Mini-mystery

Pooltime Puzzler

It was a sunny morning and I was lounging by the pool at our hotel. We had arrived in Florida yesterday and were taking it easy. The drive to Florida had taken longer than usual because we got stuck in a roadblock on the way down.

My dad was in the pool, splashing around with my little sister Louise. My mom was stretched out on the lounge chair next to me, reading a book.

"Plunk." A tall woman with flaming red hair and long, sparkly earrings sat down in the chair on the other side of me.

"How ya doin', darlin'?" she asked in a slow drawl. "I'm visiting my son, who moved here last year from our home state of North Carolina."

"I'm here with my mom and dad. . .and my little sister," I said.

"Oh, a sister," the lady said, "that's nice. Girls run in my family, too. I don't have a brother, but I do have a sister, who has no children." She continued, "My sister's father had a wife whose mother had a great grandaughter with a twin sister. But the twins had no brothers."

Across the pool, someone yelled to the lady. "Peaches, I'm ready to go."

The lady smiled, got up, and said, "It's a nickname my son has for me. You know, like the nickname of my home state. Now you have a nice visit down here and take care of your little sister."

She walked away and I turned to my mom: "The lady with the red hair has a lot of imagination. But she doesn't have a son and she isn't from North Carolina."

Do you know how I figured this out?

dot-to-dot . . . .

Down Under

Connect the dots in order from 1 to 87 to find out what's pulling the carriage.

Skiing double

Can you spot the two skiers that are exactly alike?

Up, Up, Up, & away!

Word Search Grid:

```
                    U
          P J E T   T W
          E L S I   I A
          E G T O   I S
          S N I T   G G
          O E M G   A N
          T H A A   N I
          E B T T   I
R A D A R T E K C I T E E W W E A T H E R W E R C
I A I R P O R T C L O U D S S C H E D U L E L D B
P I L L O W F F O E K A T U R B U L E N C E W O R
T I P K C O C E N I L R I A L U B T H G I L F E Y
O E M I T L A N D I N G M I P L A V I R R A H O P
                  N D E R E
                  K E O P A
                  R C F L N
                  F L A A U
                  R Y R N T
                  E I R E S
          Y K S G N I Y L F N G
          H I G N A V I G A T E
          H I D E P A R T U R E
          N T O S S L N I B A C
              S T G H E
              A S K A Y
              P I L O T
```

Word lists (in clouds):

flying
gate
hop
hub

clouds
cockpit
crew
departure
estimated time of arrival
flight

jet
landing
navigate
passenger

seat
sky
snack
tags
takeoff
ticket

aisle
airline
airplane
airport
arrival
bags
cabin

peanuts
pillow
pilot
radar
row
schedule

time
turbulence
weather
wings

All of the words listed in the clouds are hidden in the airplane.
Look across, down, up, backwards, and diagonally to find them.

Where's my mummy?

You're lost in the museum.
Can you find your way from the dinosaurs to the gift shop?

Enter Here

World of TOMORROW

GIFT SHOP

Hide and Seek

These kids are playing hide and seek in their hotel room. Can you spy these items hidden in the room with them: a magnifying glass, umbrella, snake, hot dog, skateboard, baseball cap, book, and donut?

Flag Code

Use the International Flag Code to solve the riddle below.

A B C D E F G H I J K L M

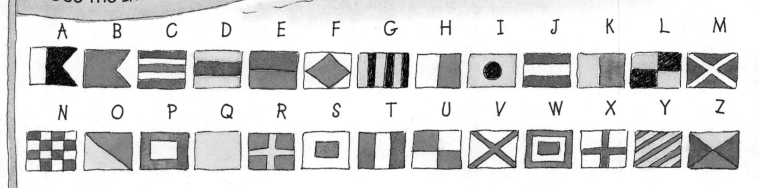

N O P Q R S T U V W X Y Z

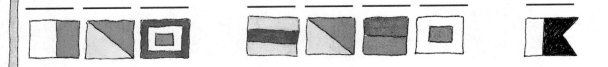

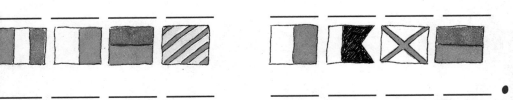

Where oh where?

The pictures below appear somewhere in this book— but where? Find each picture and write the title of the page it appears on in the blanks. The first one is done for you. Then write the circled letters in order at the bottom of the page to decode the hidden message.

1. P i c t u r e   P (a) r k

2. _ (_) _ _ _ (_) _   _ _ _ _

3. _ _ _ _ (_)   _ _ _ _ _   _ _ _ _

4. _ (_)(_) _ _ _   _ _ _ _ _ _   _ _ !

5. _ _   (_)(_)(_) _   _ _ _ _   _ _ _ _ _

6. _ _ _ _ _ _ (_) _

7. _ _ _ _ _   _ _ _ _ (_) _ ?

8. _ _ _ _ (_) _ _   _ _ _ _ _ (_)

9. _ _ _ _ _ (_) _   _ _ _

_ _ _ _   _ _ _   _ _ _ _   _ _ _ ?

Road-Tested

I Spy

If you are "it", choose an object, like a red button, and say: "I spy with my little eye something red." The other players then take turns trying to guess what the object is. The person who guesses the answer gets to be "it". HINT: Don't give the answer away by staring at the object.

Name That Tune

Players take turns thinking of songs and humming them for one another, a few notes at a time, while the others try to be the first to "name that tune." Once you have a tune in mind, hum just the first three notes. If nobody recognizes it, hum the first four notes. Keep adding notes one at a time until someone guesses the name of the song. The first person to guess becomes the next "hummer." (Good whistlers can whistle their tunes.)

Make Me Laugh

This game is serious fun. No kidding! One person becomes the "jester" and the rest are "stonefaces." Stonefaces must never laugh or smile—if they do, their faces break. Of course the jester thinks this is funny and likes nothing more than to make stonefaces crack up. That's the game! The jester has to crack up the stonefaces. The jester can make faces, funny noises, tell jokes, but cannot tickle or touch the stonefaces to make them laugh. The last stoneface to laugh gets to be the next jester.

City Train

If you know the names of a lot of cities, take a ride on the City Train. The rules are simple—players take turns saying the names of cities. The only catch is that each city name must begin with the letter that ended the last one. For example, Houston might be followed by New York, which might be followed by Kansas City, and so on. Any player who can't come up with a city has to get off the train. The last one riding the City Train is the winner. All aboard!

Rochambeau

This game, sometimes called "Rock, Paper, Scissors," works best with two or three players. These are the rules—paper (flat hand) covers rock, rock (fist) breaks scissors, and scissors (move first two fingers like a scissors) cut paper. All players put their fists out together to the beat of Rochambeau (Ro-Sham-Bo). On "Bo," each player forms either rock, paper, or scissors. Then everybody has to follow the rules.

Travel Games

A—My Name Is . . .

Here's a "fill in the blank" game that works its way through the alphabet. It's best when the pressure of keeping the rhythm going makes players work especially hard. Here's how a boy might start things off beginning with the letter A: "A—my name is Abner, my sister's name is Anne, we come from Alaska and we sell Axes." A girl might follow, "B—my name is Bertha, my brother's name is Bert, we come from Boston and we sell Beans. You get the idea—you're out when you can't complete the sentence or when you break the tempo.

Buzz

If you've got a head for numbers, buzz is for you. First, players pick a number from 2 through 9. That number becomes *buzz*. Once *buzz* is named, players take turns counting, starting with 1. If *buzz* is 3, whenever you get to a number that contains a 3 or is a multiple of 3, you must say *buzz*. Players who mess up are out, and counting starts over again from 1. The last player remaining wins. For a challenge, play bizz-buzz, picking two numbers instead of just one. One number is *bizz*, and the other is *buzz*.

Plate-O-Grams

This game has no winners or losers—just some funny messages. To start, somebody has to spot a license plate and read the letters on the plate to everyone. For example, the letters might be "B-R-G." Next, everyone thinks of a three-word message beginning with those letters. In this case, people might come up with "Big Round Globs" or "Beware Rabid Gerbils." (You might want to allow "little" words so the plate-o-grams make more sense, for example, "My Brother is Really Gross.")

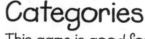

Categories

This game is good for many ages, since it can be made as easy or as difficult as you want. It all has to do with categories. One person thinks of a category—any category. It could be colors, capital cities, sports teams, or anything you can think of. Then players take turns naming items in the category. The game ends when someone repeats something already mentioned or when players can't think of any other items in the category.

Alphabet Derby

This is a race to the end of the alphabet. To play, you must find all the letters of the alphabet—in order. Letters may be found on road signs, billboards, bumper stickers, license plates, etc. You don't have to announce each letter you find, but if asked, you must tell what letter you are on. If challenged, you should be able to say where you saw your letters. The first one to Z wins. (To make things go more quickly, you may want to agree that Q is the only letter that can be found out of order.)

20 Questions

This old standby is simple, but fun. One player thinks of something (anything you can see, smell, hear, or touch) and tells the others if it is animal, vegetable, or mineral. The others take turns asking "yes-or-no" questions to try to figure out what it is. At any time a player may use a turn to guess what it is. It's best to ask a lot of questions before you start guessing, but remember, you only have twenty questions. Whoever guesses right wins. You can play this game using other categories, too, like famous people, places, or whatever—be creative!

The Twelve Days of Our Trip
(to the tune of "The Twelve Days of Christmas")

On the first day of our trip this is what I saw—
the baby throw up in the car.

On the second day of our trip this is what I saw—
two pick-up trucks and the baby throw up in the car.

Third day:
Fourth day:
Fifth day:
Sixth day:
Seventh day:
Eighth day:
Ninth day:
Tenth day:
Eleventh day:
Twelfth day:

three dead skunks
four minivans
five backseat fights
six broken headlights
seven miles of road work
eight cars a-speeding
nine railroad crossings
ten roadside rest stops
eleven cop cars hiding
twelve bumper stickers

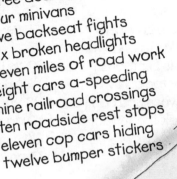

Your Destination: 99 mi.

Songs to drive

Backseat Border Blues
(to the tune of "This Land is Your Land")

This side is my side; that side is your side.
Let's get along now; this is a long ride.
You see this line here—please don't cross over.
One side for you and one for me.

I had my eyes closed—faked I was sleeping,
So you got greedy and started creeping.
Try that again, Bub, and you'll be weeping.
One side for you and one for me.

Just like I warned you—now you are crying.
And Dad is angry—now you are lying.
You had it coming, there's no denying.
One side for you and one for me.

99 Miles to Go on Our Trip
(to the tune of "99 Bottles")

99 miles to go on our trip.
99 miles to go.
Step on the gas. I think we can pass.
98 miles to go on our trip. . .

(Keep repeating until you get to
"0 miles to go" or until someone
kicks you out of the car, whichever
comes first.)

the grown-ups CRAZY!

Are We Lost?
(to the tune of "Are You Sleeping?")

Are we lost? Are we lost?
Yes we are. Yes we are.
Someone get a map out. Someone get a map out.
Find the way. Find the way.

(Save this one for when you *really* get lost. Sing it as a round—as you drive around and around—and you're sure to drive the grown-ups crazy.)

Don't Get Out of the Fast Lane
(to the tune of "Take Me out to the Ball Game")

Don't get out of the fast lane.
Don't let up on the gas.
I can't believe all the cars we've passed—
Wherever we're going, we're going there fast.
And its zoom, zoom, zoom down the freeway,
But don't break the speed limit please.
Or the friend-ly Highway Patrol
Will request your keys!

Battle Hymn of the Brat
(to the tune of "Battle Hymn of the Republic")

Our minivan is loaded to the roof with games and toys.
We've all had snacks and found a station everyone enjoys.
The kids are all behaving well; we've hardly made a noise.
But something's not quite right.

(Chorus)
I'M NOT HAVING ANY FUN YET.
I'M NOT HAVING ANY FUN YET.
I'M NOT HAVING ANY FUN YET.
THIS TRIP IS DRAGGING ON.

We've hit every tourist trap from Maine to Monterey,
Miami to Mount Rushmore, Plymouth Rock to Frisco Bay.
We wait in never-ending lines forever and a day.
It's time to take a rest.

(Chorus)

Now you might think that I'm spoiled, that my attitude is bad.
You wouldn't be the first if my complaining makes you mad.
In fact you'd be the third, behind my Mother and my Dad.
But I still feel like this:

(Chorus)

When-You-Get-There

Paper Airplane Games

Find some paper and follow the paper airplane instructions. Then you can play games with your paper planes. 1) Go for distance. Whose plane can fly the farthest? 2) Fly for accuracy. Who can land closest to a chosen target? 3) Stay aloft. Whose plane can stay in the air the longest?

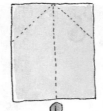

Fold, then unfold on ①

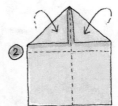

Fold down corners
Fold down on line ②

Fold down corners again

Fold little flap up

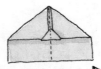

Fold this side back to meet other side

Fold wings down on both sides

Hide the Doohickey

Any small object will do in this game that is fun for kids of all ages. One player hides the object while the others wait in another room. Players are then called back to find the object. Younger players might need to be told if they are "warm" or "cold." The first player to find the object gets to hide it next.

Bright Ideas

If you have a flashlight, you will never be bored again, at least not until you wear the battery out. Set up a flashlight in a dark room and make hand shadow figures on the wall. Tell a scary story while projecting a spider or a ghost onto the ceiling. Cut out shadow puppets and put on a show. With more than one flashlight, you can play flashlight tag after dark—instead of tagging people, you hit them with your beam of light. A flashlight can also add a scary touch to face-making. Turn out the lights and see how scary you can look!

Learn to Girn

Face facts, faces are funny. Take your face to a mirror and see just how funny it can get. Serious face-makers call it "girning." It's even funnier if you have someone else to girn with. Work on blinks, winks, sneers, grimaces, grins, eyebrow raises, sidelong glances, or whatever. How many emotions can you show? How many faces can you make?

Games

Wastebasket H-O-R-S-E

A wastebasket makes a good indoor basketball hoop, and horse is a good indoor game. In horse, players take turns shooting for the hoop from various places on the court. Use rolled-up socks, crumpled-up paper or an appropriate indoor ball. If a player makes a shot, the next player must make it, too. One miss, and you get an H; two misses, an H-O; and so on. Miss five times and you are out with H-O-R-S-E.

Sock Soccer

This game is just like it sounds. Roll up some socks, set up some goals, agree on a rule or two, and start kicking. (WARNING: According to the American Sock Soccer Association, using lamps and plants for goalposts can get you in an awful lot of trouble!)

Slo-mo Volleyball

If you have any balloons left over from the water balloon toss, fill one with air for this slow motion, indoor version of volleyball. Play on your knees using a bed, couch, or some chairs for a net. You give up a point when you hit the balloon out, let it touch the ground, or fail to get it over in the agreed upon number of hits. Spike it, Dude, but don't let it pop!

Water Balloon Toss

In this damp contest, players pair up and form two lines facing each other. Each pair gets a balloon. One at a time, one person in each pair tosses the balloon to the other. After each successful toss, the tosser backs up a full step. The pair completing the longest toss wins and gets to stay dry! Most grown-ups will insist that you play this game outside.

Whirly-Bird

Make a simple paper helicopter using the instructions. Decorate your whirly-bird with markers or crayons before you cut it out. Drop your whirly-bird from a high place. When the wind is right, your whirly-bird will stay in the air for a long time. Watch it land, and then be sure to get it and fly it again.

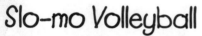

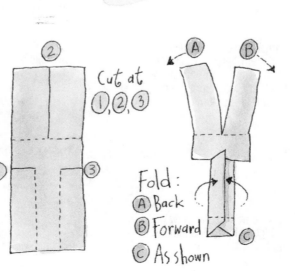

Cut at ①, ②, ③

Fold:
Ⓐ Back
Ⓑ Forward
Ⓒ As shown

Fold up

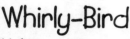

Answers

Don't miss your flight!

Travel time
1. C; 2. A; 3. H; 4. F; 5. B;
6. D; 7. E; 8. G; 9. I

Picture park

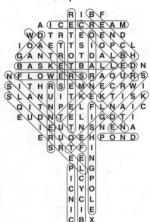

You're bugging me!
"Drop some crumbs for us!"

Summer Vacation Crossword Puzzle

Tip-Top Travel Shop
There are 30 things that begin with T: table, tablecloth, tackle box, tag, tapes, taxi, teapot, teddy bear, teeth, telephone, ten (on a price tag), tennis racket, tent, thermometer, thermos, thumb, tickets, tie, tools, toothbrush, towel, toys, trees, tricycle, trunk, T-shirt, Tuesday (on calendar), turtleneck, tuxedo, and typewriter.

Make me a map
1. B; 2. J; 3. D; 4. K; 5. M; 6. E; 7. G; 8. O; 9. C; 10. A; 11. H; 12. F; 13. I; 14. L; 15. N

Auto Repair
1. steering wheel; 2. hood; 3. accelerator; 4. trunk; 5. windshield; 6. brake; 7. dashboard; 8. wheel; 9. gearshift; 10. engine; 11. headlight; 12. bumper; 13. muffler; 14. battery

Something's Fishy

Surf's Up
1. beach umbrella is inside out; 2. lifeguard is facing the wrong way; 3. man in water is dressed in evening wear; 4. fisher is fishing with a rake; 5. skier is skiing without a boat; 6. people warming up at a campfire; 7. golfer on the beach; 8. people playing volleyball with a football; 9. sailboat has an upside-down sail; 10. in-line skater on the sand

Wacky Water park
1. park hours on sign are only at night; 2. no rungs on slide ladder; 3. alligator in the fountain; 4. pterodactyl in the sky; 5. inner tube slide spills out onto a golf tee; 6. big pair of glasses on the inner tube slide ramp; 7. queen in the lifeguard chair; 8. ice skater skating on the pool; 9. bed in the pool; 10. playing card lying on the deck; 11. herd of sheep in the picnic area.

on the right track

bloomers
1. buttercup; 2. pansy; 3. snapdragon; 4. carnation; 5. foxglove; 6. daisy; 7. cowslip; 8. goldenrod

Pathways
Michelle should take trail 1, Juan trail 2, and Keisha trail 3.

Winter Vacation Crossword Puzzle

Mini-mystery: Highway Robbery

The man in the convertible wasn't telling the truth because he couldn't have driven from Salt Lake City in Utah to Chattanooga in Tennessee in 12 hours.

Happy Camper?

Message in the sand

"Say this three times fast: She sells seashells by the seashore."

Barnyard Scramble

1. dog; 2. cat; 3. cow; 4. toad; 5. duck; 6. goat; 7. crow; 8. goose;
9. mouse; 10. horse; 11. robin; 12. rabbit; 13. raccoon; 14. squirrel

Wait for me!

The race is On!

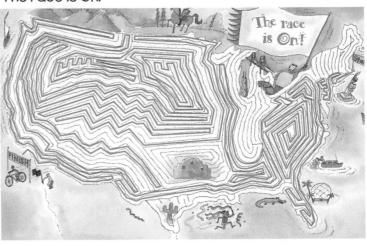

Movie Set Match-up

1. F; 2. G; 3. E; 4. D; 5. H; 6. A; 7. I; 8. C; 9. B; 10. J

Plane Challenge

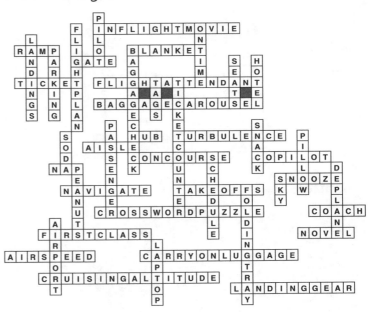

Bicycle Mix-up

1. large bike's seat is backwards; 2. yield sign is upside-down;
3. spokes missing on small bike; 4. center line on road is weaving;
5. tree growing in middle of road; 6. zebra; 7. airplane flying upside-down; 8. sun in front of cloud; 9. cow in distance is as big as the house; 10. no straps on backpack

Buy & Buy

You can buy a necklace, polished rock, postcard, wind-up toy, and candy for exactly 205 tickets. Or, you can also buy a key ring, candy, giant pencil, and postcard for exactly 205 tickets.

Which hotel?

The Sleep Inn is the correct hotel.

Zany Zoo

Soup's on!
1. peanut butter and jelly; 2. taco; 3. macaroni and cheese; spaghetti; 5. hamburger

Stormy Seas
1. ark; 2. ship; 3. raft; 4. canoe; 5. yacht; 6. kayak;
7. barge; 8. tugboat; 9. gondola; 10. sailboat;
11. submarine; 12. windsurfer; 13. aircraft carrier

A few pointers

Scattered suitcases

Mini-mystery: Pooltime Puzzler
The lady couldn't have a son. She explained that she only had a sister. That sister's father (her father) had a wife (her mother) whose mother (her grandmother) had a great grandaughter (her daughter, since her sister has no children) who has a twin sister (also her daughter) who has no brother. If her daughters have no brother, she couldn't have a son. Also, North Carolina isn't the Peach State, Georgia is.

Skiing double
Skiers B and H are exactly alike.

Up, Up, & away!

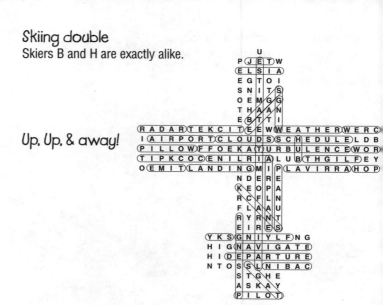

Where's my mummy?

Hide and Seek

Flag Code
"How does a country vote for a new symbol? They have a flag poll."

Where Oh Where?
1. Picture park; 2. Travel time; 3. Wacky Water park; 4. You're bugging me!; 5. on the right track; 6. bloomers; 7. Happy Camper?; 8. Barnyard Scramble; 9. Travel tips

"Are you there yet?"